FuturesTradingSecrets.com

PRESENTS

THE TRUTH
ABOUT
DAY TRADING
SYSTEMS

12 Tricks That Smart Traders Use To Make Fortunes In The Futures Markets

Bill McCready

www.FuturesTradingSecrets.com
www.FuturesTradingRoom.com

COPYRIGHT NOTICE

CONTACT THE AUTHOR

If you would like more information about this book, bulk purchase discounts, Bill's trading course, booking Bill to speak for your event or to perform a tele-seminar or webinar for your audience, please visit the author's website:

www.FuturesTradingSecrets.com

LEGAL DISCLAIMER

IMPORTANT NOTICE: Futures and Options trading have large potential rewards, but also large potential risk. You must be aware of the risks and be willing to accept them in order to invest in the futures and options markets. Don't trade with money you can't afford to lose. This is neither a solicitation nor an offer to Buy/Sell futures or options. No representation is being made that any account will or is likely to achieve profits or losses similar to those discussed in this training course. The past performance of any trading system or methodology is not necessarily indicative of future results.

DAY TRADING INVOLVES RISKS &
YOU CAN LOSE A LOT OF MONEY

Hypothetical or simulated performance results do not represent actual trading. No representation is being made that any account will or is likely to achieve profits or losses similar to those shown. By viewing this page 1 acknowledge that I have read the above statements and am aware of the risks associated with trading. Venture Planning Associates Inc. acts as a marketing agent for this training program. It does not warrant or represent that the material is accurate or will increase trading profits for anyone purchasing or using this product. All charts and techniques are provided for training purposes only.

CTFC rule 4.41 - hypothetical or simulated performance results have certain limitations. Unlike an actual performance record, simulated results do not represent actual trading. Also, since the trades have not been executed, the results may have under-or-over compensated for the impact, if any, of certain market factors, such as lack of liquidity. Simulated trading programs in general are also subject to the fact that they are designed with the benefit of hindsight. No representation is being made that any account will or is likely to achieve profit or losses similar to those shown.

A PERSONAL MESSAGE FROM THE AUTHOR, BILL MCCREADY

Thanks for picking up this book. While my ideas are free, they are priceless if you put them to work for you. I wish I had known these concepts when I started trading over 20 years ago. So, I'm no stranger to success. I have earned degrees in mathematics, engineering-physics and nuclear engineering. I've worked as a nuclear submarine officer, astronomical engineer, venture capital consultant and Internet entrepreneur. I have owned 11 businesses including a nuclear engineering company, Novell Networking Company, Hawaii Venture Capital Fund and an AM-FM radio station. Frankly, I made money at every one of these careers. Then I started trading and my winning streak hit a dead end.

It wasn't until I put together all the principles covered in the Futures Trading Secrets System that I turned my trading career from barely making it to making serious money. I ran approximately 200,000 tests of indicators, settings and time frames to develop my own system. I only decided to sell it because I was sick of so much high priced junk on the market.

I studied, experimented, tried other systems and finally worked out all the quirks for a system that even a beginner could learn and start using in a short time. If this book just grabs your attention and you want to improve your trading or get into day trading, act now. See what our students are saying at my **FuturesTradingSecrets.com** website. My charts are simple; my system is easy to use; and, you can learn it quickly if you're focused and committed to learning how to trade.

Bill McCready

Bill McCready, Founder
FuturesTradingSecrets.com
FuturesTradingRoom.com

TABLE OF CONTENTS

LET'S GET STARTED

Did you know that 15,000 websites sell day trading systems for stocks and commodities? If so many people are getting into day trading, why would you want to get into trading? Simple. Ninety percent of those traders are consistently losing money! That means there's money left on the table. Money you could make.

If that many sites claim to train day traders yet turn out 90% losers, you don't have to be a math genius to know that something isn't working. Could it be the training? Trying to teach a newbie to day trade without actual, successful trading experience is foolish and frankly, unethical.

But let's face it, anybody can put up a site on the Internet, set themselves up as an "expert" and charge big money to teach you what they don't really know. That's why so many day traders waste money to learn so little and then go into the market and lose so much.

Are You Tired Of The Hype?

Do you want the TRUTH about Day Trading? I'm talking about the TRUTH that will show you how to make money with MAXIMUM LEVERAGE. And I know what I'm saying. You see, I already put my money on the line, over and over, as a day trader for over twenty years. No magic, no false promises, I'm going to give you the straight TRUTH about day trading and the skills required.

For more information and charts of our system, visit:
www.FuturesTradingSecrets.com

TRUTH #1: MILLIONAIRES ARE MADE IN DAY TRADING

Yes, that happens, just not everyday, and not without a system. Hitting it big occasionally is pure dumb luck. If you want to rely on luck, go to a casino where you get dinner and a show while losing your shirt. Successful day traders are in the game for the long haul. They clearly understand Maximum Leverage as the key to building great fortunes. Day traders, like entrepreneurs, real estate investors and global marketers, know that the fastest route to achieving financial goals is leverage.

Are you using leverage to maximize your money? Check each of these types of leverage that you should regularly use.

- **Other people's money ...**

- **Other people's expertise ...**

- **Other people's ideas ...**

- **Other people's research ...**

- **Other people's time ...**

- **Other people's work ...**

- **Other people's mistakes ...**

If you are not using these types of leverage, what are you waiting for? Get busy using at least three of these types of leverage right now to move toward your financial goals faster and with less stress on you. My proven leverage building approach begins with 5 Key Methods:

1. Find an experienced Mentor ...

2. Identify tools and skills used by experts ...

3. Incorporate checklists that advance the system ...

4. Connect with a Support Network ...

5. Develop a Mastermind Group ...

Briefly let's look at how these five methods work together to build leverage.

1. **An experienced Mentor teaches what he or she already knows how to do.** A mentor has perspective from years of actually day trading, plus proficiency gained from developing an effective trading system. An experienced mentor has the patience to guide you in day trading without throwing you in too soon or micro-managing your trades. Take time to find the right match for your mentor.

   Take time to network with the experts at seminars and investor meetings to identify a potential mentor. Then make sure the mentor or "mentee" relationship is a two-way street in which the mentor receives equal value in return for guiding you toward success.

2. **You need a good quality computer and a high speed Cable or DSL Internet connection plus a large flat screen monitor.** Higher resolution, larger monitors are easier on your eyes. They help you focus on charts and important market indicators. If you prefer a lap top computer to a desktop, a compromise is a docking station so you can enjoy the larger monitor when at your desk. Master Chefs think nothing of spending a thousand dollars for their knife sets and the best hair stylists spend hundreds on a single pair of scissors. The

tools you need to become a money-making day trader are not inexpensive. Price, however, is not always an indication of the depth of training you will receive.

3. **Before NASA launches a space shuttle, dozens of people run through exhaustive checklists for every critical item.** Who could remember all of those things with the anticipation of a launch? When you are day trading, you can get caught up in the intensity of the market and forget key factors in your system. Master traders use checklists every day. They would not think of trading without the checklists that keep them within the parameters of their system. Your mentor can show you how to develop or adapt checklists to use with your trading system.

4. **Trading is a solo activity that takes you away from the group and focuses on your trading system.** Do that too long without hearing new ideas and you become painfully isolated. Staying connected to a support group helps you to maintain a positive attitude as well as listen to other people question some of your ideas that need more work. You may find the right support in an investors group, local business organization or among friends.

5. **A Mastermind Group is a "Dream Team" of like-minded people who share your passion for achievement, know the sweet taste of success and have skills worth sharing.** Group members can work together to identify trading opportunities, analyze charts and review each others' portfolios. A Mastermind Group operates as a unit in which each member is expected to participate, offer ideas and contribute to the group success. Mastermind Groups are not for traders who want to leech ideas off others without giving back.

The bottom line is that Maximum Leverage is the fastest way to build wealth. Before you trade, secure these **5 KEY ELEMENTS** to get fully prepared.

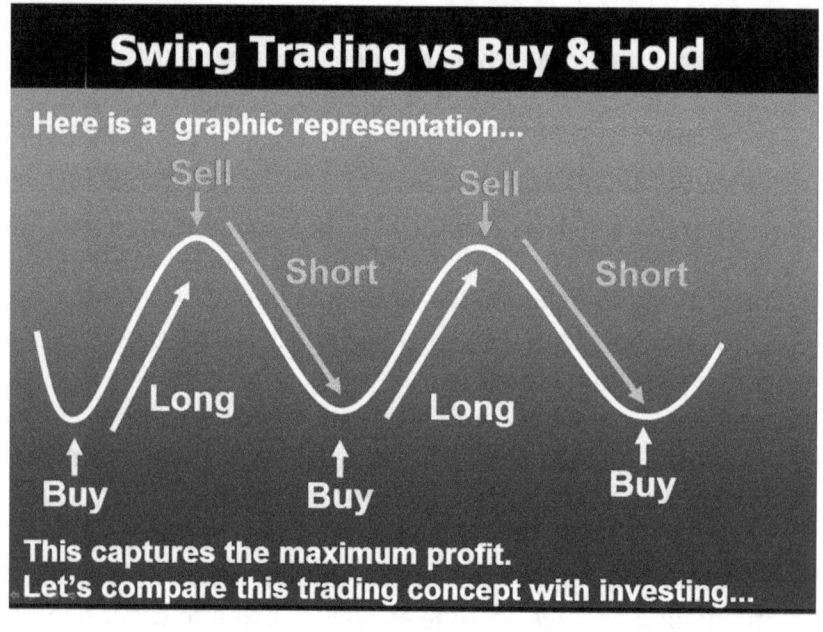

For more information and charts of our system, visit:

www.FuturesTradingSecrets.com

TRUTH #2: TRADING IS THE PERFECT BUSINESS

Day trading is the perfect business if you really understand it. As strange as this may sound, trading is the least risky way to make money that I have ever experienced. Where else can your $500 control $50,000 in value and risk only $50-$75 per contract traded? That kind of leverage is unparalleled in any other financial vehicle. Even more amazing is that trading is a business with:

- **Low startup cost** – computer, Internet access ...

- **Low overhead** – work at home, by the pool, at the coffee shop ...

- **No permits or licenses** – trading for yourself is not a regulated business, no expensive annual business permit ...

- **No set hours** – trade when you want, as many hours as you choose, take breaks when you choose ...

- **No self-employment tax** – just Capital Gains tax ...

- **No employees** – no payroll, forms, supervision, or irritation ...

- **No selling** – no products, services or neighbors running from your latest pitch ...

- **No inventory** – no stuff to stock, service, insure, sell or tie up your capital ...

- **No advertising** – with nothing to sell, there's nothing to advertise ...

- **No real estate** – no tenants, termites, trash or evictions ...

Those are the general business advantages and there are still greater advantages to trading stock indexes such as the eMini S&P, the Russell 2000, DAX, Hang Seng, Nikkei and Forex markets.

- **No steep learning curve** – except, you do need to know yourself and how to handle emotions ...

- **No worries about market direction** – profit short/long anytime ...

- **No individual stock shocks** – a general market sentiment ...

- **No interest charges** – you put up the margin first ...

- **No restrictions** on markets to trade ...

- **No restrictions** on time frames to trade ...

- **No fears of inflation or recession** – you can weather both of these conditions and make money while others complain ...

- **No big transaction fees** – $5-$10 per contract ...

- **NO BOSS** – Total freedom to make all your own decisions!

The indexes smooth out all the news shocks except major world or national issues and allow you to trade the psychology of how the world feels about your current economic situation. As you probably know, 90% of all mutual funds never beat the indexes. So why not trade what works best? The indexes are the most liquid and easiest market to trade with the best leverage.

TRUTH #3: RISK IS PART OF TRADING

E very trader looks for the infallible signal. That's like the search for the Holy Grail, the hunt for Red October and the August vigils at Graceland where crowds of faithful expect Elvis to walk back into the building. You might as well wait for the next Halley's Comet. At least that's predictable. So stop looking for some astounding signal.

There simply is no fool-proof signal to trade. Even if a fool-proof signal for trading existed, 90% of the traders would still miss it because they are relying on an emotional reaction to some mystical occurrence. Every trader has to operate in the same environment of unknowns and probabilities. You must have a realistic edge in the market. That edge, in my opinion, is belief in a positively biased system and the belief, patience and discipline to follow it.

Programmed mechanical trading systems claim to take the emotion out of trading and deal strictly with facts. The problem is that mechanical trading systems are discretionary systems that have been hardwired, over-optimized and geared to only one type of market. Mechanical trading systems lack flexibility to respond when markets change without warning.

To give you a head start in the market, here are some of my prime tips for controlling risk in trading. Pay attention, these tips are worth thousands.

- Know your risk level – calculate carefully so that you risk a maximum of 2-5% of equity per trade:

- Preserve your capital at all costs ...

- Stops are NOT the same as money management ...

- Increase trade size on winners ...

- Decrease trade size on losers ...

- Catch mistakes and get out immediately ...

- Never, NEVER add to a losing trade ...

- Indexes and FOREX allow leverage up to 200% so be cautious ...

- Remember – leverage works both ways; high rewards come from high risk ...

- Disaster Stops must be set to avoid adverse reactions to global events that rock financial markets without warning ...

The other thing about risk is that if you have a profitable money management system that you believe in and TRUST, you will dramatically reduce your risk. *(See Truth #5)*

Start small and build your faith and belief in your system. Trade larger until you feel uncomfortable with the risk. You have now discovered your intuitive risk tolerance. Back off a few contracts and concentrate on hitting singles and doubles (to use a baseball metaphor). The home runs will come, but don't swing for the fences every time. Consistency is the key to becoming very profitable.

TRUTH #4: THE MARKET MOVES; THE ISSUE IS WHEN, NOT WHY

Some traders try to find out whether people in the market or people outside the market have the greatest impact. Who cares? As a trader you need a system to identify market moves regardless who or what influences it.

Actually, it is people sitting on the sidelines, but their impact is nearly impossible to measure. At any given time, there are ten times as many traders and a hundred times the capital sitting on the sidelines waiting for who knows what. This represents the force and energy that causes market movement. If the market is in equilibrium at a fair price, then price is stable.

What happens in any corner of the world can have an impact on our financial markets. This "Chaotic Reaction" to a minor event can cause massive movements almost instantaneously. In other situations, the market moves totally counter to what conventional wisdom thinks will happen based on news global events. Meanwhile, traders caught on the wrong side of the market must liquidate and reverse or face huge losses, further accelerating the move. That's why you see radical short term moves in various indexes and the FOREX markets.

Just as the paparazzi are trying to guess which drug rehab facility to stake out for the next celebrity photo, thousands of traders waste as much time trying to figure out what other traders are going to do. If you want to monitor other people's actions, become a paparazzi or a nosey neighbor. Successful traders have no time for this.

The truth is that all the information you need to know about the news, the effect of the news, what traders think of the news, and what professional traders think other traders are going to do is already reflected in the last few price bars on any chart. It is so simple that all you have to do is watch the price chart and understand what the chart is telling you NOW.

No matter what happens, the market is always searching for equilibrium. Getting there is what makes for the ups and downs of trading. Traders with a solid system can ride the market waves with the same exhilaration and triumph of a champion surfer hitting the Banzai Pipeline.

LEARN THESE PRINCIPLES OF MARKET MOVES

- Constant testing of highs and lows is just part of the market.

- Failure happens when the market does not exceed the high or low by less than one or two ticks.

- If a recent high is exceeded in a Breakout, the next logical place to test is the last high before the test and then a test of the breakout high in a retracement.

- Continued tests and failures lead to Decreasing Trading Ranges and a Triangle Formation. While the market awaits news, **delay trading** when the range decreases too much.

- Daily Logic that says a market is going toward a new high will hit a low first. The opposite is also true.

All trading is probability based. Traders are not prophets so their ability to predict market movements is limited. You can increase the odds in your favor by looking at short term trades and momentum.

Here is an example of the testing of Support and Resistance, Pivot Points, and Fibonacci numbers with our custom indicators. Here are six instances where the market turns at these points. We use these as targets only. Other signals are used for entries and exits.

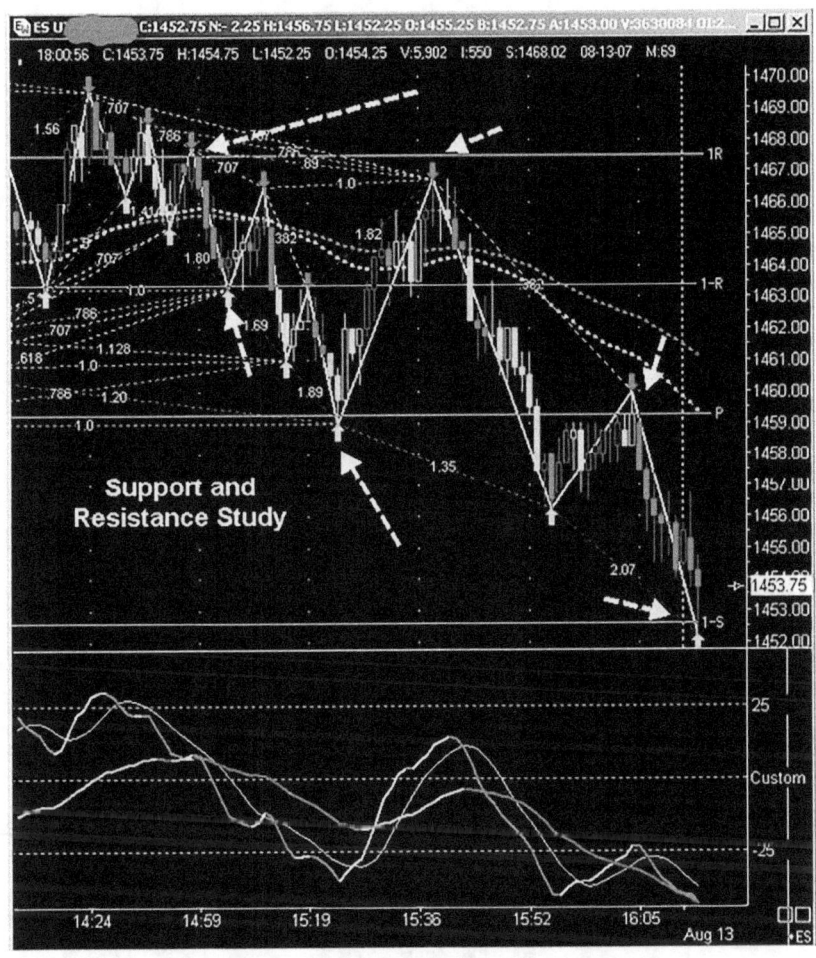

"Support and Resistance Study" Chart

TRUTH #5: MONEY MANAGEMENT IS THE KEY TO PROFITABLE TRADING

Most trading systems miss the all important aspect of Money Management. Making money is great. Keeping it is even better!

An important element of preparing to trade is reviewing your financial situation and establishing a reasonable amount of money to place at risk. Pay the mortgage, the electric company, car payment, insurance premiums and other necessary living expenses first. Set aside some money in reserve as an emergency fund, at least enough to carry you through a short term crisis. Then, and only then, are you ready to determine the amount of money available for trading.

Next, you need to gather sufficient data to outline the type of market to trade, the maximum acceptable risk, and proper capitalization of your account and the expected win-loss ratios of your trading method. Ready to trade? Not yet. You need to practice turning profits with a SimBroker until you are ready to jump into the real market with your REAL CASH or you won't have any money left to manage.

Over trading or trading too large for your account size (plunging) is the downfall of many traders. Hoping for a trend change is the second downfall. Trade what you see, not what you hope to see the market do.

Here is a day that would have driven most traders straight to the bar of their choice. Eighty percent losers, but wait! Proper money management, stops, exits and patience lead to a profit at the end.

It is also an example of overtrading on a SimBroker. Money Management helps you make money, but your Broker made more than you did because you over traded.

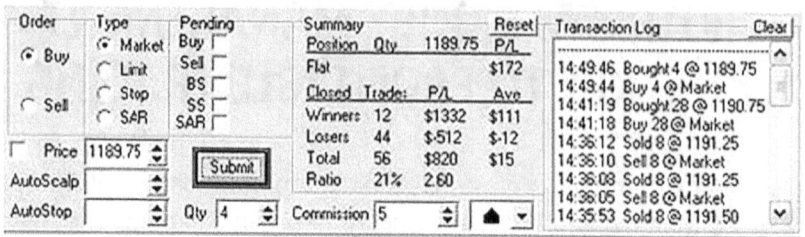

Try to take only "Loaded Trades" and never take more than three trades a day.

Making money is short lived if you don't know how to manage what you make.

So, we suggest that you take money out of the market and off the table as soon as you can so that you are only playing with the market's money and not your own.

For more information and charts of our system, visit:
www.FuturesTradingSecrets.com

TRUTH #6: BEFORE YOU TRADE: PRACTICE, PRACTICE, PRACTICE

Your piano teacher was right – practice makes perfect. Of course, there are no perfect musicians and no perfect traders, but there are "virtuosos" in both fields. Extensive practice with a simulated trading program is how you practice a trading system. If you don't have access to a simulated trading program with a broker or charting system, we use and recommend the SimBroker from Ensign Software. The SimBroker and the Demo feature allow you to download data for up to two months prior data for all indexes and then allows you to replay this real time data at two to ten times higher speed. You can get in a week's trading practice in one night.

Note: We recommend Traderbytes or DTN IQ feed and Ensign for our trading. It does make a difference which data and charting program you use. My choice is always for the best tools if you are going to trade with your money at 100 to 1 leverage.

We use tick charts rather than time charts so it is very important that the data be correct. We tried many data feeds over the years and settled on Traderbytes because their data comes directly from the market; not so with many others. Traderbytes has been voted "best data" by traders for over 12 years.

1. Ensign was designed by guys who have been trading for more than 40 years.

2. You get free updates at least twice a month so you get all the latest stuff.

3. Ensign does tick charts better than anybody including eSignal.

4. Ensign has a Demo feature that allows you to download actual

market data from the past three months and then replay it at 2-10x speed to practice trading.

5. Ensign also has a built in SimBroker that dings you 1/4 point on market orders, allows bracket trading, and you can use it against both the Demo data and the actual market.

6. Ensign has some special indicators that are great early warning signals for exits and market turns.

7. Because we recommend you practice until you get to 70% hit rate with at least a 2/1 win loss ratio, this has helped all of our students do much better in the market.

8. One thing, Ensign allows you to use several data feeds, so you do have a choice if you need to use a satellite.

DO NOT CHEAT

You can play all types of games on a SimBroker and all you are doing is cheating yourself. Practice as if REAL MONEY is on the line. Keep a meticulous trading log with the SimBroker from the very beginning. This will highlight your progress and definitely show your weaknesses. Your goal is to get to a 70% correct trading call ratio with at least a 2/1 win to loss ratio.

The SimBroker dings your account for commissions and slippage just like the real market. Forget cheat codes. There aren't any. The SimBroker allows you to gain or lose based on your decisions by testing your trading skill in a real time simulation. Trading with SimBroker gives you a feel for trading and how well you perform under pressure. That's where practice makes the difference. Keep practicing until you achieve the results that establish **your trading plan.**

Here's a SimBroker screenshot with an 86% win to loss rate and a 1 to 1 profit:

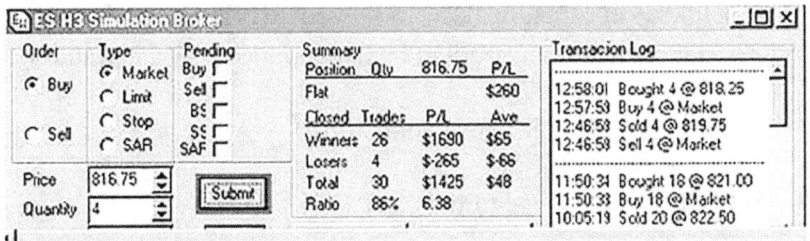

The more you practice with SimBroker, the more confidence you develop to trade probabilities and accept losses as normal. That gets you ready to implement the Expectancy Formula for your trading plan.

Start with These Essential Formulas:

Expectancy Ratio = (Probability of Win x Avg Win) – (Probability of Loss x Avg Loss)

Profit Potential = Expectancy Radio x # Trades x # Contracts x Value

Factor in a high reward, 80% probability of win with 5.4/1 risk gives this result:

(80% x 5.4) – (20% x 1) = 4.12 x 10 = 41.2 x 2 x $50 = $4,120 in possible profit ...

A losing system with high reward:

(40% x 10) – (60% x 1) = 3.4 x 10 = 34 x 2 x $50 = $3,400 in possible profit ...

A realistic system for the average trader:

(60% x 2.5) – (40% x 1) = 1.1 x 10 = 11 x 2 x $50 = $1,100 in possible profit ...

Those formulas become the basis to set your STOPS and EXITS in your Money Management and Trading Plan. Keep these rules in mind:

- Set Stops and NEVER move your stops ...

- Set Exits at the logical targets ...

- Use Disaster Stop for global crises ...

- Establish longer time frames with Support, Resistance and Pivot Points ...

Take the time to really understand what this formula is telling you. If you practice and get to a positive expectancy and you can actually execute the trades, then you have an absolute winner of a system.

Many systems we have seen promoted actually have a negative expectancy. If they advocate a 2-point loss and a 1-point gain, you can calculate it yourself. You actually need to win over 67% of the time just to break even!

TRUTH #7: THERE IS NO PERFECT INDICATOR

ndicators are treated like fads by some traders. Ninety percent of ineffective traders vacillate between this indicator and that one and then move on to another one. Indicators can alert, confirm or predict price movements depending on the settings. Concurrent time frames are the secret to high probability signals. Choosing useful indicators is definitely a sophisticated process and I've already gone through the range of possibilities. You can benefit from my trial and error.

Without a doubt, indicators can be misleading. In a classic Stochastic trading system, the signals are given by crosses of the 20% and 80% lines. Depending on the settings used, you may get vastly different signals. The primary function of indicators is to smooth the price.

All indicators use a mathematical process to make price easier to understand. In some cases, this creates divergences that give early warnings of a market turn or flattening. To get the most from indicators follow these tips:

- Apply a combination of Leading and Lagging Indicators ...

- Keep all indicators in the same time frames ...

- Avoid multiple indicators using the same data or you can get a false sense of security ...

- Include Long Term, Medium Term and Short Term ...

- Avoid Collinear Indicators that measure the same thing ...

- Most indicators are variations of the same principle. Select two or three indicators that you understand and develop expertise in using them for your trading system. Use a maximum of five indicators of different types. Choose one from each of the first four following possibilities. The last category is only for overall daily analysis and is not much help.

1. Trend Indicators – MACD's, ADX, Moving Average Systems ...

2. Volatility Indicators – Bollinger Bands, Envelopes, Keltner Channels

3. Momentum Indicators – MACD's, MACD's Histogram, Stochastic, Relative Strength, Williams%R, CCI, RSI ...

4. Cycles – Fibonacci Retracements, Fibonacci Time Cycles, Pesavento Patterns ...

5. Market Strength Indicators for volume or open interest – Money Flow, Volume, On Basis Volume, Advance Decline, TRIN, TICK, and TIKI ...

How do I make indicators work in my trading? I use three simple indicators for a setup. Signal 1 is early and a warning. Signal 2 is a non – lagging indicator (not listed here). Signal 3 is a confirmation of the direction of the indicated. The fourth indicator is simple logic.

The example charts on the next page show you an overly complex chart and a chart used in my system. (Shameless Self Promotion)

For more information and charts of our system, visit:
www.FuturesTradingSecrets.com

POPULAR SYSTEM WITH 10+ INDICATORS

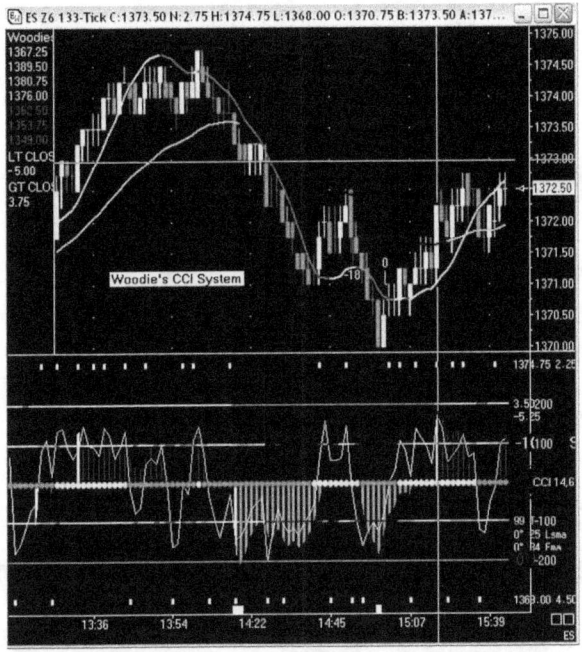

Futures Trading Secrets Chart with 3 Indicators

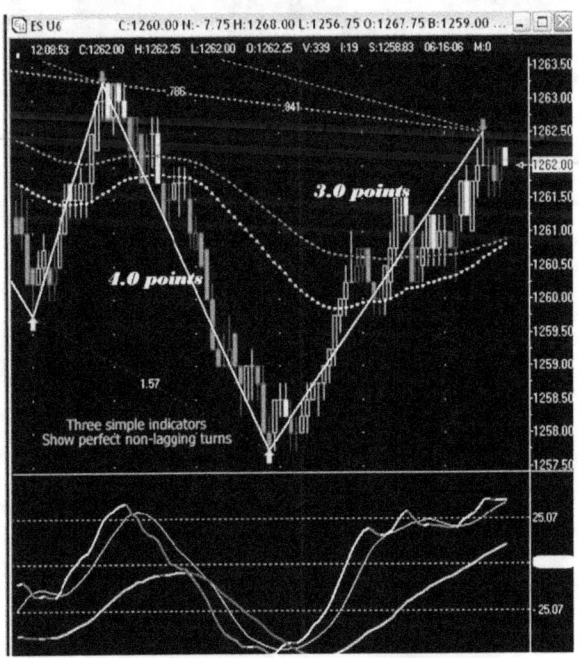

Our 3 Indicator System

TRUTH #8: THE MARKET TURNS ON SUPPORT & RESISTANCE

Remember that the market always seeks equilibrium. It's the macro logic of the market that results in oscillation between previous highs and lows. You can expect the market to test the most recent opposite support or resistance. With that in mind, you need to review a medium term and daily chart to see the longer term support and resistance areas.

In dealing with support and resistance, follow these principles:

- Pivot Point is the setting used rather than the close on each bar because it is the most representative price. The formula to calculate Pivot Point is (High + Low + Close)/3 ...

- Trend Reaction numbers of Support and Resistance are calculated from the Pivot Point. For example, the First Resistance Level is calculated as follows: $R1 = (P \times 2) - L$

- Always mark Globex High and Low on your chart for reference. The test of these numbers also occurs in the first hour of trading.

- Weekly Support and Resistance provide reliable Price Envelopes for buying and selling ...

- From the Daily Pivot, look to sell at Previous Hi, Globex Hi, Rally High or Resistance ...

- From the Daily Pivot, buy at Previous Low, Globex Low, Decline Low or Support ...

- From Daily and Weekly Retracements, look for standard Fibonacci retracements and confluence of daily and weekly retracement on the current chart ...

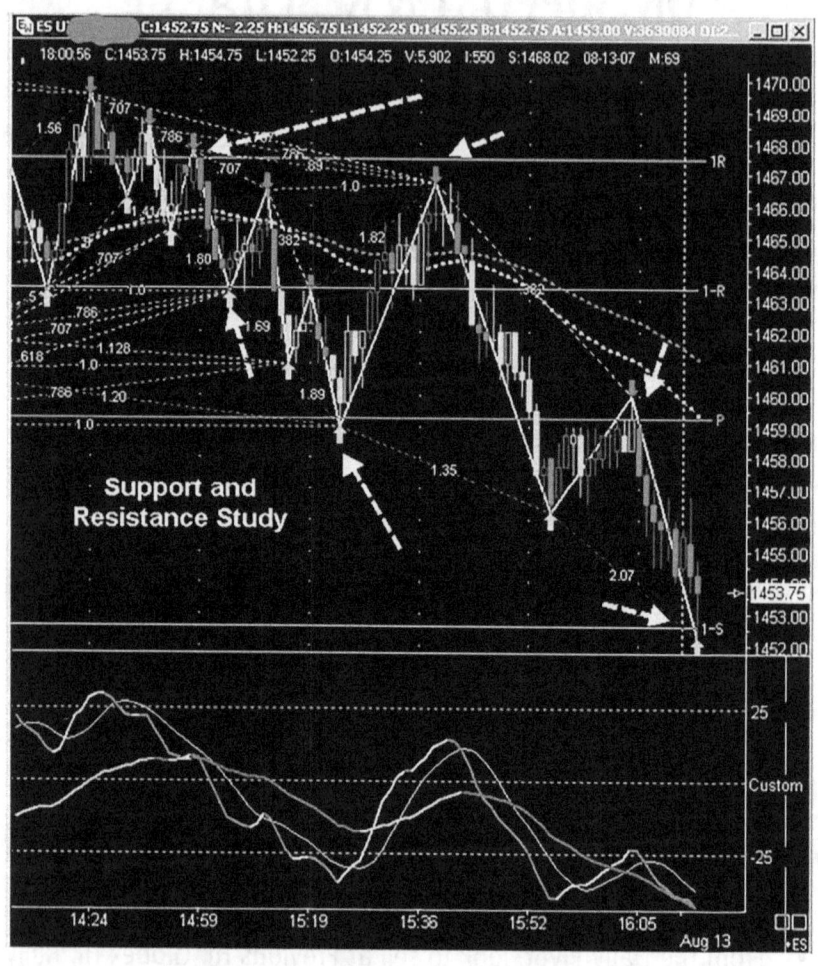

"Support and Resistance Study" Chart

How to Calculate Pivot Points

There are several different methods for calculating pivot points, the most common of which is the five-point system. This system uses the previous day's high, low and close, along with two support levels and two resistance levels (totaling five price points) to derive a pivot point. The equations are as follows:

- $R2 = P + (H - L) = P + (R1 - S1)$

- $R1 = (P \times 2) - L$

- $P = (H + L + C) / 3$

- $S1 = (P \times 2) - H$

- $S2 = P - (H - L) = P - (R1 - S1)$

Here, "S" represents the support levels, "R" the resistance levels and, "P" the pivot point. High, low and close are represented by the "H", "L" and "C" respectively.

Support and Resistance levels are price targets, the points where we stay out of trades if not currently in the market. Many traders play these levels but it's tough to predict high and low on our probability list for making money. If you have a successful trade with a profit, get out when approaching a significant Support or Resistance level. Sit out the volatility and wait until the market decides which way to move.

There are also minor Support and Resistance levels and turning points to be aware of daily. The market simply goes up or down and then retraces to the most recent high or low as a test.

TRUTH #9: FEAR WILL DEFEAT MORE TRADERS THAN ADVERSE MARKET CONDITIONS WILL ... EVERY TIME

There's a saying, *"Fear is a mind killer!"* Even President Franklin D. Roosevelt stabilized an anxious post-Depression nation with the admonition, "The only thing we have to fear is fear itself." Trading can be a roller coaster experience with exhilarating highs and heart pounding, spirit sagging lows. No question fear is a persistent enemy that plagues every trader.

The best weapon against fear is facts. That's why you need a dependable trading system, checklists, indicators and charts. These are factual sources. But these numbers are only flat marks on a paper until you interpret them. That's where the emotion creeps into the trading process. With all the mixed signals from trading programs, so-called gurus, time frames and more, it's hard to separate fact from fiction. Until you settle on a trading system and work that system consistently, you will second-guess yourself into bankruptcy by hesitation, frantic moves or total freeze up. Reactive trading is fear based trading, and a sure way to lose your shirt and your sanity.

From a trader's perspective, you need to understand four facts about fear:

1. Fear can be explained as False Evidence Appearing Real. If you are going to expend anxious energy, make sure there is a reason.

2. Fear does not stand up to knowledge. When you prepare, analyze and plan, fear is replaced by positive energy.

3. Fear of the unknown has no place in trading. Unless you thrive on meeting challenges, testing your skill and accepting the unknown

as part of the process, then trading is not for you.

4. Fear of failure is tied to a frantic effort to predict the future. You can make intelligent assumptions with indicators and charts, but you will not be right every time. No trader hits every signal, every time.

Going into the market without a solid system is unquestionably a reason to be fearful, and trying too many systems leads to "Paralysis of Analysis." Find a system that takes the fear out of trading with solid education and simulated experience and then stick with it. Using SimBroker, you know what it feels like to win and to lose. You also learn to respond to changes effectively and what happens when you allow fear to overcome reason.

> **Belief in a trading system begins with total understanding of what you are trying to accomplish and your motivation. Then you need to believe in each separate part of the system and personal practice to "lock it in." Fear is overcome with familiarity, and confidence comes from recovery from unknown and unpracticed bad trades, as well as good ones.**

TRUTH #10: NOTHING HAPPENS UNTIL YOU PULL THE TRIGGER

U nless you "pull the trigger" and execute a trade, you are an observer not a trader. Every trader feels apprehension and then moves on. If you are stuck with your hand literally hovering over the execution button, what's stopping you from pulling the trigger? Go back and read *Truth # 9 (Fear)* until you understand how it affects you.

Traders wait too long to pull the trigger because they are waiting for that perfect moment when all indicators are "go." Re-read *Truth #7*. Psychologists will tell you that the flip side of perfection is procrastination. No kidding. Procrastinators are perfectionists who cannot make a move until everything is lined up exactly as planned. In the market, perfectionists/procrastinators are more likely to be observers than traders. Even if the perfect indicator occurs, would you recognize it? Traders learn to trade by trading. It's that simple.

When it's time to pull the trigger, some people hold back because:

- Greed takes over good sense. Instead of taking a reasonable profit and getting out, they wait for more and lose big.

- Substituting "gut feeling" for analysis and indicators. It may just be indigestion.

- Trying to get too close to a significant support or resistance level is like dancing at the edge of a fire. You are likely to get burned.

- Spending more time chasing new theories and programs than trading is only profitable to the program sellers.

- Fear of winning is as great a problem as fear of losing. What if you make a big profit? Was it a fluke or was it skill?

- Simulation is safe, so some would-be traders get too comfortable with pretend trading to risk real money.

- If you are just too afraid to pull the trigger, admit it to yourself. Quit trading and do something more productive with your life than stare at a screen all day.

Your trading education should be geared to trading, first in simulation and then on the live market. Any other course of action is totally worthless if you never use the knowledge and practice to actually trade. One thing that no one can do is pull the trigger for you.

I can tell you one thing with absolute certainty ... when you conquer fear, greed, perfectionism and procrastination, you will pull the trigger with confidence!

TRUTH #11: A SUPERIOR SYSTEM STANDS UP TO RIGOROUS EVALUATION

Let's face it, the Internet offers hundreds of trading systems. Most of them are full of hype and storytelling. Many of these systems were created on the fly by people who have little or no actual trading experience. You could learn just as much by reading articles online and save your money, but then you would have to figure out how to put it all together. I know because that's how I learned and believe me it's the hard way.

Another fault of some trading systems is that you become dependent on the guru or the next newsletter or paying for consultations on each trade. That's not teaching you how to trade. A superior system works, and when you learn it, you can make it work for you.

I want you to use these guidelines to evaluate any trading system. Charlie Wright wrote a great book about trading systems a long time ago. Here is a summary of how to do it yourself.

- You need a minimum of 50 ticks (market trades) in a bar chart to have a statistically significant system

- The largest winning trade must not exceed 50% of total gross profit or 25% total net profit. Otherwise it could be random luck that skews the results of the system.

- You need to have a positively biased Expectancy Ratio of the system. If it does not exceed 2 to 1 with 50% probability factor, you will lose money due to slippage, commissions, and all the variable and fixed costs of trading.

- Back testing is not a valid testing method. You need to evaluate the trading rules going forward and taking every trading signal. You cannot "Cherry Pick" the system trades.

If the winning percentage is less than 50% yet still makes money, then the question is, can you psyche yourself up to trade it and live with all the losses in order to follow the system? Market wizards like Van K. Tharp, Mark Douglas, Bill Williams, and Bent Steenbarger say that **you trade your beliefs about the market.** You must know your risk tolerance, your ability to take a trade where the future is unknown, and how you react psychologically to wins and losses.

How do you acquire a solid trading system and make it your own? You start with a goal that leads you to the results you desire. Then you find a superior system that teaches the basics while allowing practice opportunities in a simulated market environment. Before you actually trade in the market, you develop a plan to achieve your goals that honestly considers risks, rewards, and processes to achieve your goal.

Once you use the system in the real market, you experience what it means to execute the plan, closely monitor the results and make incremental changes as needed. The final step is to check your emotions to see if you can actually trade the signals and play the probabilities for gains (rather than losses). If you can't trade your system, you will never achieve your goals. That's a guarantee!

TRUTH #12: THE TECHNIQUE OF EFFORTLESS & PROFITABLE DAY TRADING IS ...

I want to share some thoughts on how to become a better trader. A method that seems too easy, but it uses a method that does not involve driving you crazy searching for the Holy Grail or beating yourself up for missing another trade. Often we are just plain trying too hard instead of just trading.

Day trading is a skill, like sports, you need to have goals and objectives, but when you are trading (or playing), you need to leave those things at the door of your trading room and just trade.

All sports teams want to win. They all pray to win and they all know they are the best team, but sometimes even the good teams lose. They get ahead and then get too conservative or they are way behind and almost catch up. Often you will hear "we tried our best but ..." Trying is not doing. As it has been said before, "There is no try, only do or not do."

Is this losing syndrome just fate, an unanswered prayer, or is it something different? Are you lacking in the old Attitude, Belief and Commitment taught by so many motivational speakers? Are you missing the critical point of the book, *The Secret*? Or is it something else that is very easy to understand, but not easily implemented? Actually, you already know the *Secret*. It is just that no one ever really pointed out to you that you already know it.

At the end of this section there is a secret to automatic action without emotion that will make you a better trader, golfer, skier or poker player. If you skip ahead you will miss it and fail miserably, so be patient and disciplined. Let's get started.

33

First, all of you have probably read the Mark Douglas classic, *Trading In The Zone*. In his book, he defines these Five Fundamental Truths of Trading. For audio interviews, go to **FuturesBlogger.com** and search my blog topics for Mark Douglas.

1. "Anything can happen." My comment — Never assume anything when a short-term trade is on--never move your stop to a greater loss — ALWAYS move it tighter if the market moves into your profit territory but doesn't quite give you your profit target. If this happens, then take what the market gives you. The last tick or two is the costliest tick or two in trading — it has blown out smaller traders' accounts when ignored.

2. "You don't need to know what is going to happen next in order to make money." My comment — Trading is most likely — in the purest sense — probability based. Trading is also position sizing based on the strength of your signal, coupled with an efficient and properly timed entry. This requires iron-clad discipline after entry according to exit rule parameters a trader should know without fail.

3. "There is a random distribution between wins and losses for any given set of variables that define an edge." My comment — To minimize "emotion," trade contract sizes you are comfortable with. Use your edge, and you should consistently utilize a timeline that allows you to trade that size with a risk that you are also comfortable with. If you get nervous in a trade because of the open profits or a trade nearing your stop loss, you are simply trading too large for the moment.

4. "An edge is nothing more than an indication of a higher probability of one thing happening over another." My comment — Statistically over time, with practice and a minimum of errors, this is exploitable for consistent capital gain, given the right mindset, trading capital and temperament for short-term trading.

5. "Every moment in the market is unique." My comment — Without

a doubt, just ask an S&P floor trader or long time trader. Market participants are in and out constantly and their seemingly random trades change the internal dynamics of the market constantly. You must learn to be only in the NOW. It is that simple.

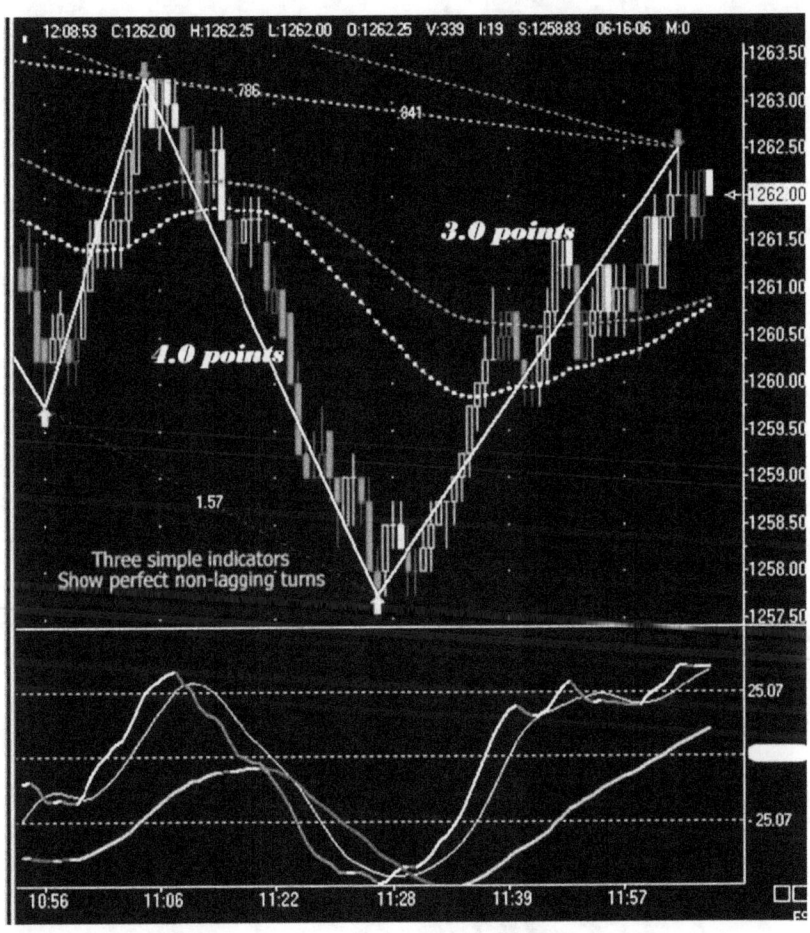

OTHER THOUGHTS & COMMENTS

Market wizard, **Mark Weinstein, wrote,** "When I trade at home, I often watch sparrows in my garden. When I feed them bread, they just take a little piece at a time and fly away. They keep flying back and forth, taking small bits of bread, which is the way to day trade. Better to take your little sips from the giant ocean frequently a few times a day and then be done — in the day trading markets."

Isn't this the attitude most short-term traders should adopt? My mentor, Chick Goslin, author of a great book, *Trading For A Living*, once told me that we get what we want out of the markets. If it is emotional ups and downs and attitude and hope and cheerleading and ego, you'll get shredded. You need to be in this for the money and freedom, which **always requires iron clad discipline, patience, and relaxed concentration.**

All of these statements boil down to using **the real secret to making money in the markets.** That is if you are in this to make money and not for the fun or imagined sport of day trading. **Here is the secret.**

When the market gives you money, take it! Take little bites of the pie, and you would be surprised how quickly they add up. Like the golf saying, "Drive for show and putt for dough." **Trade for dough!!!**

Golf is very much like trading. You NEVER GET THE SAME SHOT TWICE. Different courses, different times of day, different slopes, distances, wind, grass, trap sand, etc, etc, etc. These variables sound like the market to me.

I was in the bookstore the other day waiting for my car to get serviced, so I decided to read as many diverse books as I could on learning a new skill. One book that caught my eye was Timothy Gallwey's book, *The Inner Book of Golf*. Years ago I had read *The Inner Book of Tennis* and it totally changed the way I thought when playing sports. Tim's message way back then was: "Play! Don't Think." I was curious to see if he had changed his tune, but no, he was still on the same message.

It turns out, he was going to test his own mental approach toward teaching himself to be a golfer. He had given up golf for teaching and tennis and had not touched a club for 25 years. So who did he interview? Al Geiberger, the first pro to ever shoot 59 in a PGA golf tournament. That record stood for over 25 years. Al Geiberger's teaching video, produced by the Stanford Research Institute, was a series of slow motion shots of Al hitting balls. No talking, no instruction, just shot after shot with quiet music in the background.

Timothy spent the time interviewing him on his mental state when playing. Al's secret: He doesn't think, he PLAYS golf, he hits the ball, and he putts. If he thinks about his swing, his grip, his posture, where he wants to put the ball or his score, he loses his concentration.

Sounds a bit like trading. Thinking too much about rules, signals, how much you have made or lost, the car, your bank account or anything else causes you to lose concentration. In fact, the best way to 'game' a golf partner who is cleaning your clock is to ask him to show you his swing or his putting technique. Tell him he is going to set a personal best round ever and he will blow up. I guarantee you his next shot will be out of bounds or in the water. (You can use this technique in any sport and it always works.)

Tim goes on to talk about how we learn sports skills and points out the two standard methods.

1. **Mechanical Teaching Programs** that talk about mechanics use all those incredibly funny tools (the movie *Tin Cup* comes to mind

here), and tons of books and pictures. Not too effective, because if it were, there would be no more books on golf (or trading).

2. **The Feel Approach.** I have shared this concept with many of you. It is how you learned to play ping pong or cast a fishing lure. This is the Inner Approach. You build muscle memory and you correct things until you get it right. That is how I learned golf. People who learned golf this way are pros like Lee Trevino, Jim Furyk, and Arnold Palmer. If you look at their swing, it is awful and not at all the "classic swing" of a Tiger Woods. However, they all are great golfers, and are not going to change their swings to conform to some artificial rule of how you should swing. They simply hit the ball and play golf.

So here is the question: **Which needs to come first? Experience or Mechanics? The answer is they must come simultaneously or neither is very effective.** You have to get in the game, on the court, or in the pool and get a feel for the environment before any of the mechanical teaching tools have any real meaning.

Repetitively practicing the wrong technique will ingrain bad habits that take years to undo. Reading too many books leads to overwhelm. So what is the secret that Tim Galway discovered? Simply that both of these approaches work, but they are slow and tedious.

Galway has another method basically focused on **Awareness of What Is Happening Now** and **Effortless Effort**. I won't spoil the book(s) for you, but this is the Holy Grail for learning any sport, or trading. Here is a tip.

Keep your conscious mind occupied so your subconscious can control the action.

If you read between the lines, that is what all the great traders, market wizards, Zen Masters, and master craftsmen, Michael Jordan, Tiger and all those "in the zone" are saying. That is why I recommend using a meditation MP3 or listen to your favorite instrumental music while you are trading. I like Jazz because it is unstructured. My friend and long-time trader, Norm Hallett has an excellent website on this topic.

This method will also control your emotions while trading. If you can, find a hobby that absolutely rivets you outside of short-term trading and puts your emotional ups and downs, your attitude and your ego into that hobby. It will most likely balance out an itchy trigger finger or the pulling-the-trigger hang ups you are having trouble with now.

This principal is also the genius of the little book that I highly recommend *Blink: The Power of Thinking Without Thinking* by Malcom Gladwell. You should be able to walk by a computer, take the first trade you see without thinking (assuming you have practiced and can recognize a signal in the process of forming) and then exit and walk away. Your subconscious, the smartest, fastest, computer in the universe makes the decision without YOU (reads "your ego") in the blink of an eye.

Come back in a few minutes and see what actually happened. You will be amazed at how easy and how often you are right with that trade.

One last golf story and I will switch to tennis, swimming or skiing. I studied Aikido for many years and found a golf teacher who was a 5th Degree Black Belt, LPGA Teaching Pro, National Women's Junior Champion, etc. Jamie Zimron became a friend and playing partner while I lived in San Diego. On her 50th birthday, Jamie played an incredible 212 holes of golf on a difficult course in San Diego and averaged 75 per 18 holes for the whole day by playing fast and without thinking.

NOW FOR THE SECRET I PROMISED YOU

Here is a little test you can run yourself. Using the SimBroker, use your usual trading style, analyze, worry, fret, think, hesitate, jump the gun, and take 100 Trades with the SimBroker and record your results.

Next, I want you to take 100 trades and exits with the Blink Technique. Make sure you leave the SimBroker running after a trade, get up, go away for a few minutes to clear your mind and then come back and take the very next trade you see.

Record the results and see what happens. Trading this way and trusting your subconscious can have amazing results and give you great confidence. Send me your results. I know this test will help you be a much better trader, because you will stop over analyzing and just trade. It will be effortless and you will not be agonizing over every entry and exit.

There are multiple books written on this principle, by sports figures like Tiger Woods, Michael Jordan, and in the trading world, you have Mark Douglas, Brent Steenbarger, Marcel Link, and all the Market Wizards speaking about the same concept. Historical and legendary traders like George Lane of the Stochastic Indicator and Gerald Appel of MACD fame all made fortunes using a simple system they understood and could trade automatically.

So practice, practice, practice and practice some more until you get a system or see a signal that is automatic. If it is not mine, then develop your own, but get into the automatic mode with your trading as soon as you can.

Bill McCready,

Bill McCready

www.FuturesTradingSecrets.com
www.FuturesTradingRoom.com
www.FuturesBlogger.com

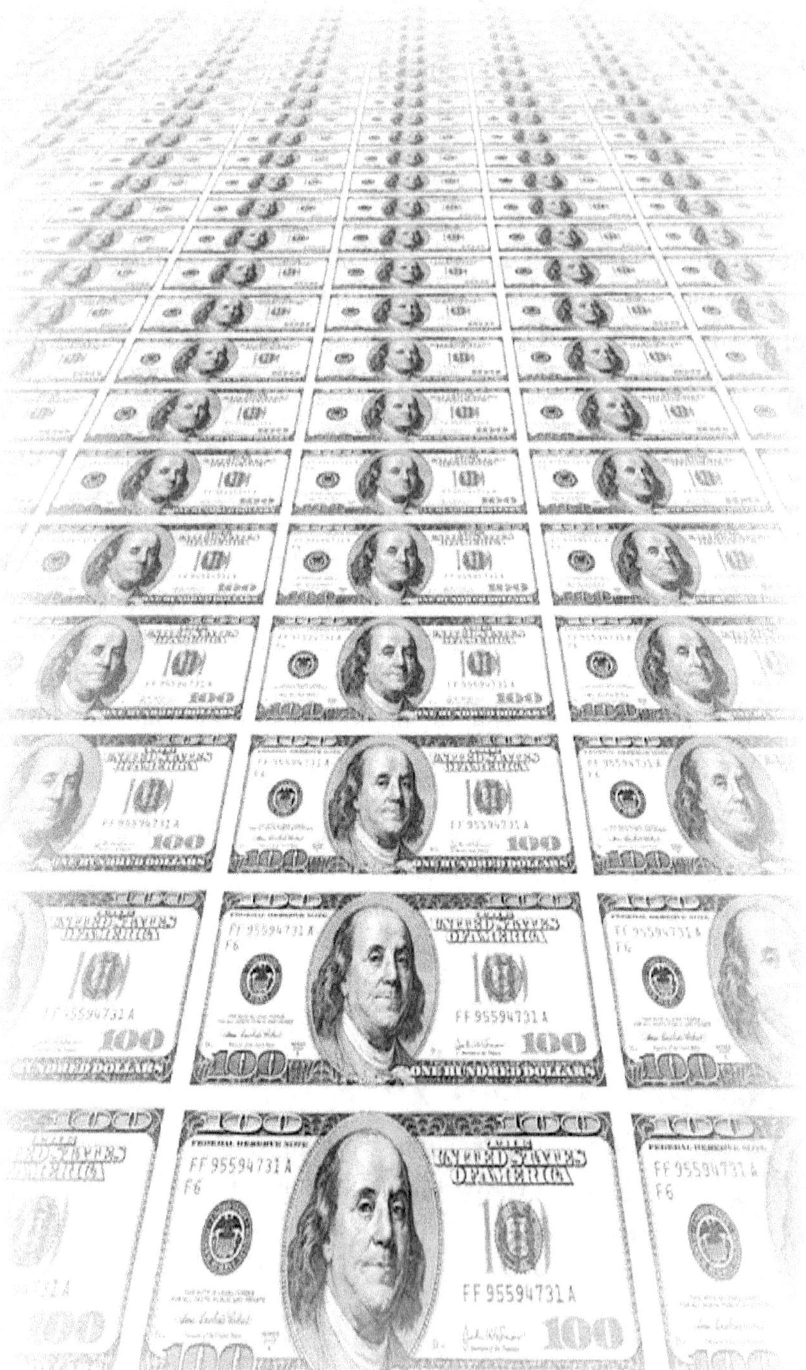
FEDERAL RESERVE NOTE
UNITED STATES OF AMERICA
FF 95594731 A
F6
100
ONE HUNDRED DOLLARS

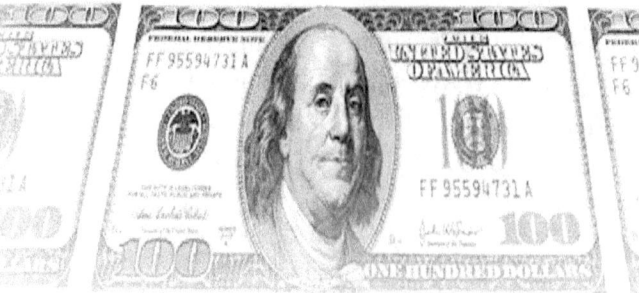

ABOUT THE AUTHOR

DON'T WASTE 6+YEARS LEARNING TO TRADE!

Who is Bill McCready and why should YOU take this book seriously? I thought trading would be easy! I am a smart guy, but did not become a successful trader until I understood all of the principles covered in my *Futures Trading Secret* system. My name is Bill McCready and I was the typical loser in the stocks and commodities trading gamee. Until I started to trade, my life was one success after another. I am now in my 70s and started trading about 20 years ago with only limited success. I had a few big wins and lots of small losses.

I have degrees in mathematics, engineering-physics and an M.S. in nuclear engineering. I've worked in management positions as a nuclear submarine officer, astronomical engineer, venture capital consultant and Internet entrepreneur. I have owned 11 businesses, including an engineering company, Novell Networking Company, AM-FM radio stations, an international product trading company, and a venture capital fund and consulting company.

I am the creator and originator of this system and program. I have learned from many people, but the total package is my creation and how I trade. Why a Futures Trading Secrets Course? I spent upwards of $50,000 to learn how to trade. Now I am sharing what I have learned in my **Futures Trading Secrets** course so YOU don't have to invest that much to learn a successful way of trading.

Check our learning curve, the programs that helped, and others that did not help. YOU can save a lot of time and money by taking our course. See what my students say at my website, **FuturesTradingSecrets.com/testimonials**.

While thousands of traders and trades contributed to the development of this system. it is not a Holy Grail system, but a method of looking at the market in a different way and a way to make YOUR own decisions and set YOUR own risk levels. **The bottom line is that this method works for me and it can work for YOU!**

IMPORTANT DISCLAIMER NOTICE
DAY TRADING INVOLVES HIGH RISKS & YOU CAN LOSE A LOT OF MONEY

Commission rule 4.41(c)(1) applies to "any publication, distribution or broadcast of any report, letter, circular, memorandum, publication, writing, advertisement or other literature, "commission rule 4.41(b) prohibits any person from presenting the performance of any simulated or hypothetical futures account or futures interest of a CTA, unless the presentation is accompanied by a disclosure statement.

The statement describes the limitations of simulated or hypothetical futures trading as a guide to the performance that a CTA is likely to achieve in actual trading.

Commission rule 4.41(b)(1)(i) hypothetical or simulated performance results have certain inherent limitations. Unlike an actual performance record, simulated results do not represent actual trading.

Also, since the trades have not actually been executed, the results may have under-or-over compensated for the impact, if any, of certain market factors, such as lack of liquidity.

Simulated trading programs in general are also subject to the fact that they are designed with the benefit of hindsight. No representation is being made that any account will or is likely to achieve profits or losses similar to those shown.

BILL'S TRADING COURSE,
COACHING & AFFILIATE PROGRAM

#1 – Futures Trading Course

Learn how to trade like Bill online at his training website, FuturesTradingSecrets.com. With over 20+ hours of online video trading instruction, trading tips, tactics, and insights only Bill knows and uses to trade, you too can tap into how Bill trades to make money in the Futures markets.

#2 – Futures Trading Coaching

How would you like personal help getting started trading in the futures market? Then, you might be interested in learning more about Bill's personal coaching program. If you're new to trading, don't go it alone. With so much to gain (financially) with trading, you have nothing to lose when you invest in yourself and one-on-one coaching with Bill.

#3 – Futures Trading Affiliate Program

Do you know people who would be interested in learning about Bill's online trading course? You might consider signing up to become an affiliate for Bill and promote his trading course to those you know. Perhaps trading is/isn't for you or you haven't had time to learn how to trade for real dollars. That's all right. Why not recommend Bill's program to your friends and associates? In doing so, you can earn commissions for every sale you refer.

LEARN TO "TRADE LIKE BILL"

"Futures Trading Secrets" Course

www.FuturesTradingSecrets.com

YOU are ONE SIMPLE STEP away from Spectacular SUCCESS as a TRADER!

Trading is 50% mental, 40% money management and 10% signals. In order to climb into the top 5% of all traders and become consistently successful, YOU need to master all THREE areas. I can help you do that.

If YOU want to master the markets and increase YOUR success, YOU need to consider the **Futures Trading Secrets** course. One thousand plus students (30% professionals) have chosen my program as their last resort/final course.

FTS Course Out Performs Professional Money Managers ...

Bill,

I have been trading YOUR system for the last eight months. I also have two managed accounts. The FTS program consistently out-performs the results of these professional money managers.

Also, with the materials and support you provide, I find that this course is complete and should help any trader improve their results.

Kudos,

Michael O.
Professional Trader
Sarasota, Florida)

STUDENT TESTIMONIAL

You can read a book or look at charts, but it is not enough. You need video training on the live market in order to trade in real time at the Hard Right Edge of the chart. That is what the **Futures Trading Secrets** course offers you ... **MORE THAN 20 HOURS** of interactive market-time training videos online for you to access 24/7/365 to help you learn all our signals fast.

Our Exclusive Dual Time Frame Trading System

Real-time videos comparing approaches to trading the eMini, include: Stochastic Indicator Systems, Dual Ergodic, Pesavento and Fibonacci Cluster Systems, including Pivot Points and Support and Resistance Levels.

My videos show YOU how and why I picked a unique set of indicators to give YOU with up to 80% accurate signals. (I estimate that I've tested over 200,000 combinations to get these settings just right for you and for me.)

The written portion of the 100+ page course includes over 69 charts, four Excel tracking and support spreadsheets, and all the trading rules for pinpoint entries and exits. Whatever I'm using, I share with you.

You get six charting templates and multiple work spaces for Ensign Software so YOU can trade exactly as I do with Indexes, Forex, Stocks and Option Swing Trades!

What is in the Futures Trading Secrets System

A simple, but very accurate trading setup that requires three signals for a setup as seen below. I call this my 1-2-3 GO SETUP for either reversal or continuation trades.

- An early warning signal to either exit or wait for signal two to enter (the arrows).
- A color change in the non lagging indicator (purple or white indicator below).
- A cross over of the non lagging indicator (the yellow line below).

See this chart below from 5/24/2012 for what YOU get with your course. All indicators, Fibonacci, arrows print automatically on Ensign and Trade Station.

PLUS YOU GET THESE 6 BONUSES!

My complete TRAINING PROGRAM includes the following BONUSES:

1. A complete method for setting up your trading business.

2. A daily trading plan and premarket opening checklist.

3. Daily mental and financial analysis tools to improve your trading including a tracking log and a risk/reward spreadsheet for self analysis of your trading.

4. A commodities risk and growth calculation spreadsheet to help you trade multiple contracts and markets.

5. A one-page entry and exit rules reference summary that is easy to implement and refer to when necessary.

Your complete dual time frame trading system with all our trading signals, is MADE AVAILABLE TO YOU IMMEDIATELY AFTER PURCHASE! This is an ONLINE COURSE you don't want to pass up if you're serious about learning how to trade like Bill!

TO GAIN FULL ACCESS TO BILL'S TRADING COURSE & START LEARNING HOW TO "TRADE LIKE BILL" GO TO:

www.FuturesTradingSecrets.com

GET TRADING COACHING

BILL'S PRIVATE TRADING COACHING PROGRAM is a proven method to rapid success in virtually any trading endeavor. Trading has many nuances, tricks and traps. There's so much to look out for when first starting out. Knowing these tactics in advance from an experienced trader can make all the difference in your personal LEARNING and EARNING curve.

An initial webinar to outline the program and get your system set up will be provided to you in advance. Following the coaching, an exit webinar will be held to review any final questions or problems.

You will receive a complete copy of the *Futures Trading Secrets* course in advance and have two weeks to study ahead of time, so you can get familiar with Bill's trading methods before you start mentoring with Bill.

Homework will be assigned that will require you to evaluate your current trading style, money management criteria, business and trading plans and a thorough understanding of the *Futures Trading Secrets* methodology.

In the second week, Bill will be online and you will make the trades or trading calls, so we can review and see if you have Bill's trading system down correctly. Private consultations to solve problems will be held with those students who need additional help.

For the following three months, you will have priority help available upon request and one-on-one with Bill.

When you choose to trade live, you do release *Futures Trading Secrets* of all responsibility for any gains or losses to your own account by purchasing this program. The trades discussed are for training purposes only and are not recommendations to take any trades. Please read the complete disclaimer again at the front of this book.

Student questions, trading logs, and annotated charts from the previous day for discussion in the current day's training session should be submitted before 2:00 P.M. Pacific Time the day before a live trading session.

IF YOU THINK PRIVATE COACHING IS FOR YOU, THEN GO TO:

www.FuturesTradingSecrets.com/coaching

BILL'S AFFILIATE PROGRAM

Join the **Futures Trading Secrets** affiliate program and make money selling Bill's online course to other futures and day traders what they need most, which is a step-by-step formula for success ... *every day they trade!*

WHO SHOULD JOIN

Business owners, managers and webmasters of stock, option and futures trading websites. Publishers of stock market or commodities related e-zines, blogs and newsletters. Owners and managers of discussion groups, forums, and chat rooms, and social networking websites related to day trading.

HOW IT WORKS

All you have to do is place a link or banner on your web site, a link in your newsletter, or a link in your signature file when you moderate or participate in discussion groups and chats. You can even include a link in the signature file you use in every email you sent out! When a visitor clicks from your link or banner to the Futures Trading Secrets (link to FuturesTradingSecrets.com) website, and orders the course, you earn a commission.

PROGRAM DETAILS: COMMISSION STRUCTURE & TYPE OF PROGRAM

Venture Planning Associates, Inc., the parent company of Futures Trading Secrets, offers a 2 tier affiliate program that pays a % commission on primary sales and an override on sales of all affiliates recruited. See website for details.

PAYMENT SCHEDULE

Commissions are paid monthly on balances of $50 and up. If in the unlikely event we get a return, we will charge that return against your next commission.

AFFILIATE SUPPORT & MARKING TOOLS

We supply you with marketing tools, banners and the support you need to promote Bill's online futures trading course.

HOW TO JOIN

To sign up and become an affiliate, go to the link below. After you fill in the online affiliate form, you'll receive your affiliate link and access to marketing banners. At that point, you can start promoting Bill's course and start making money!

www.FuturesTradingSecrets.com/affiliates

www.ingramcontent.com/pod-product-compliance
Lightning Source LLC
Chambersburg PA
CBHW070405190526
45169CB00003B/1123